WOMEN DO

Women Do This Every Day

Selected Poems of Lillian Allen

LILLIAN ALLEN

women's
P R E S S

CANADIAN CATALOGUING IN PUBLICATION DATA
Allen, Lillian, 1951-
Women do this every day: selected poems of Lillian Allen
ISBN: 0-88961-192-0
1. Women, Black - Poetry. 2. Feminism - Poetry. I. Title.

PS8551.L5554W6   1993   C811'.54   C93-095215-4
PR9199.3.A55W6   1993

Copy editor: Heather Green
Cover illustration and design: Denise Maxwell
Author photo: Patrick Nichols
Series logo: Sunday Harrison

This book was produced by the collective effort of Women's Press.
Women's Press gratefully acknowledges the financial support of the
Canada Council and the Ontario Arts Council.

Printed and bound in Canada
1 2 3 4 5   1997 1996 1995 1994 1993

Dedicated to my sister Olive and my Aunt Dolly,
two remarkable human beings whose light shone in my
life and in the lives of many others.

To Aunt Nie, Aunt Tin, Aunt Tunny, Aunt Tiny and
Sista Sugar and to my cousin John (Patsy).

To my mother and father — Thelma and Amos.

To the Spanish Town people, especially those of
French Street.

To Toronto's Black community for its vitality and
fighting spirit.

Inspiration and love due to Clifton, Maureen, Clive,
Chet, Ivan, Vera, Deanna, Sunday, Gwen, Ann and
Marrie.

Special thanks to Heather and Martha.

To the revolutionary vision of the Minquon Panchayat.

And to Anta.

Contents

Preface

Because words don't (always) need pages, I have publish-
ed extensively in the form of readings, performances and
recordings. I have been reluctant to commit my poetry to
the page over the years because, for the most part, these
poems are not meant to lay still.

As I prepared poems for this collection, I was required
to "finalize" pieces I had never imagined as final. Like a
jazz musician with the word as her instrument, reading
and performing these poems is an extension of the crea-
tive and creation process for the work. In some ways, I
had to reverse this process to "finalize" these poems for
print; finding their written essence; pages do need words.

These poems breathe, they are alive. Sit quietly with
them, read them aloud or shout them in public places.

And remember, always a poem, once a book.

Enjoy —

Lillian Allen

Introduction

By the time I was formally introduced to literature in high school, I was amazed and dazzled by the sheer festivity of the Jamaican language. To my delight, I found I was also excited with the sensuality and power of the written word — its ability to transport me to new worlds, to describe emotions that were real. Writers who wrote passionately out of their own situations engaged me the most.

Growing up in Spanish Town, Jamaica, in a British-style school system, I was conscious of the tension between how you expressed yourself in a natural, joyous and feisty way outside the school context and how you were supposed to express yourself at school. It was assumed that if you wanted to make something of yourself and get ahead, you had to leave your culture and "bad talk" behind. Very early I knew this was not an attack on "bad" culture or "bad" language. Such an orchestrated strategy to "keep these people in their place" and to stigmatize something so fundamental to a people's identity and sense of self, was a deliberate attempt to degrade and destroy the very essence of who we are. It was a first recognition that racism and discrimination are also based on social and economic realities.

Jamaica is known as the dynamic little country that gave the world reggae music. A predecessor of dub poetry, reggae music emerged from the grassroots. Its birth was an undeclared act of subversion — no invitation was issued and no permission granted. It was an authentic people's voice with a rhythm of resistance and hope. It carried a universally felt heartbeat, and a message of defiance and resistance. Reggae was associated with ignorance and lack of sophistication, and was much frowned on by the arbiters of Jamaican "taste and culture." It subverted the complex and subtle structure of censorship under capitalism, a structure maintained by the imposition of class-based and racially-biased "standards for expression." These "standards" conspire to negate, exclude and limit the possibilities of expression.

It is precisely because of reggae's success, and the nature of that success, that dub poetry developed. Reggae was relevant to the lives and concerns of ordinary people. Its stance was dignified and demanding, its messengers sincere. Without reggae, dub poetry could never have existed. And without two remarkable figures of the twentieth century, Louise Bennett (who is now living in Toronto) and Bob Marley (at rest), there would be no dub poetry.

Louise Bennett, Miss Lou, as she is affectionately known, emerged in the forties, along with outstanding poets like Claude McKay, George Campbell and many other young West Indian writers. The forties were a time of shifting political consciousness in the region. In the thirties, there had been massive strikes throughout the Caribbean, as well as massive migration to Britain. Now, along with the mobilization of various sections of the labour force, came an awakening to a sense of national identity — the potential of nationhood.

Louise Bennett developed a persona that fit in with the African tradition of the artist as preacher, teacher, politician, storyteller and comedienne. Because she lived in a society that relied heavily on spoken communication, she wrote in the language that most Jamaicans speak most of the time. And she did it long before it was acceptable. She wrote of their triumphs and pain, their follies and foolishness. But most of all, she gave them a mirror of who they are and gave them permission to be proud of themselves, and to fight back.

Ef wi kean sing "Linstead Market"
An wata come a me y'eye,
Yuh wi haffi, tap sing "Auld Lang Syne"
An "Coming thru de rye."

— Louise Bennett
"Bans O' Killing" from *Jamaica Labrish*

Miss Lou presented "problems of classification and description" for the literary establishment. Although she had been publishing books since 1942, she was not acknowledged as a writer. Despite exclusion, Louise Bennett took her words — through the medium of performance — directly to the Jamaican people. Today her books, stories and poems form a *major* document of Jamaican social history and culture. She is a stunning example of resistance, self-sufficiency, freedom and self-determination.

With the social and political movements of succeeding decades, art and culture took on a new and significant role for Jamaicans. The sixties brought the Black power movement in America and its poets of resistance (Jane Cortez,

Sonja Sanchez, Nikki Giovanni, Gil Scott-Heron, Amiri Baraka, The Last Poets and so on); the liberation from British colonial powers fanned post-independence aspirations; and the rise of the Rastafarian movement, emphasizing Black people's role in history, and a return to African roots, brought a spiritual dimension to political determination.

Bob Marley appeared on the heels of Louise Bennett. Like many of the artists of the sixties and seventies, Marley looked to Miss Lou for inspiration and used the body of her work as a reference point. He was able to build on the messages of her work and get on, in a more direct manner, with the business of calling "the system" to account.

In the early seventies in the dance halls of Jamaica, competing sound systems with highly skilled DJs and refrigerator-size speakers vied for the biggest crowds. This was the indigenous pop culture of the people and this music did not find acceptance on the island's radio stations until much later on. Star DJs — the mighty U-Roy, Big Youth and I Roy — chanted messages over instrumental versions on the flip side of popular songs. DJs were so totally marginalized from mainstream or official Jamaican culture that no subject matter and no individual, no matter how powerful, was sacred. These DJs talked about anything and everything in the society, from the private and personal to social and political taboos.

The mixers of the music or studio engineers became conscious of the way in which the live DJs worked with the music and the interactive dynamics of their performance in the dance hall context. The engineers and studio mixers attuned their techniques to create re-mixed versions of the instrumentals. The mixers' techniques of echoing, repeats, fades, dropping in and out of instruments to create internal rhythmic dynamics, ignited the imagination of a generation of young poets: Oku Onuora, Mutabaruka, Jean Binta Breeze, Mikey Smith, Nabby Natural, Malachi Smith, Poets in Unity among others. These groups of word practionnaires, all born in the early fifties, echoed the rhythms, the excitement and the concerns of the period.

It was in this period — the late seventies — that Oku Onuora first pressed the term dub poetry into circulation, describing his poetic creations and the poetic ventures of some of his fellow poets in Kingston, Jamaica. By giving it a name, Onuora inadvertently allowed the crystallization of a new and distinct poetic form. It was not just a matter of liberating poetry from the constraints of academia. Onuora expressed the deep resolve of his contemporaries:

I am no poet
 no poet

I am just a voice
I echo the peoples
 thought
 laughter
 cry
 sigh
I am no poet
 no poet
I am just a voice.

Dub poetry is not just an art form. It is a declaration that the voice of a people, once unmuzzled, will not submit to censorship of form.

Dub poetry developed simultaneously in and outside of Jamaica. It surfaced in the major metropolitan areas where West Indians migrated, especially in London, England, and Toronto, Canada. In London, poets like Martin Glen, Benjamin Zephariah and Linton Kwesi Johnson engaged their communities with their activist poetry. In Brixton's embattled Black community, Linton Kwesi Johnson set his political poems to a menacing reggae bass line:

night number one was in BRIXTON
SOPRANO B, sound system
was beating out a rhythm with a fire
coming down his reggae-reggae wire

— Linton Kwesi Johnson,
"Five Nights of Bleeding"

The working-class Johnson emigrated to England from Jamaica in 1963. He is best known for his militant poetic contribution to the political struggles of Blacks in England, and of the working class in general.

Those of us working in Toronto — Clifton Joseph, Devon Haughton, Ahdri Zhina Mandiela, Ishaka, Afua Cooper — although thousands of miles from the "source," discovered that our artistic responses to the conditions of our lives were similar. Instinctively, we set out to shape this new expression; to work with a form whose aim was to increase the dynamism of poetry, to increase its impact and immediacy, a poetic form that could incorporate many aspects of other art forms: performance, drama, fiction, theatre, music, opera, scat, acappella, comedy, video, storytelling and even electronics. It was poetic ammunition, an artistic call to arms.

When I first started to write, I wrote plays and short stories. Because it was impossible to get an encouraging word from publishers at the time ("there wasn't a market for such works") or to get a play produced, I switched to poetry. It was, to put it simply, more portable. It was like art to go. Take-out art. Me, my poetry and the public. No "middleman." But it wasn't always easy at those community meetings in the seventies where I found a captive audience for my poetry. For a long time, I was scheduled to perform during the break, when everyone was reaching for coffee, or at the very end, after six speeches, five-and-a-half of which were completely unnecessary. It was like,"Thank you folks for coming ... *la luta continua* ... we'll pass the bucket for donations (big speech on importance of donating here) ... and now sister Lillian will read some of her poetry." It wasn't easy wrestling prime time from the political heavyweights. But the audience came to love and expect the poetry and demanded it when it was not there. Even today, political events in Toronto's Black community include poetic and other cultural offerings as an integral part of articulating issues, forging collective energy and making essential connections.

From the mid-seventies, dub poets were activists working in Toronto's Black community on many issues affecting our community — racism, police brutality, racially-biased screening of Black children in the school system, the plight of single mothers in public housing, racist immigration laws and practices. We worked for the upliftment and liberation of African peoples in general. We worked to organize Black parents, for African liberation support committees and for various other solidarity causes across racial and cultural lines. We worked in white organizations and created possibilities for others. We wrote, performed the works of other poets and experimented. We believed in possibilities. That art is political. That the cause of our art, like the cause of art that maintains the status quo, must be declared openly. That art in itself is symbolic and although it can play a major role in people's lives and in social and political movements, it cannot change the structure of social relations. The work of the poets extends beyond merely creating art; we take our poetry and our convictions into the community. We organize, we network, we participate, we protest, we celebrate, we build community.

But the limitations of a Black nationalism that has macho tendencies, that defined political, social and personal problems solely along racial lines, coupled with the patriarchy of the male-dominated white left, made it imperative for women to raise issues of women's oppression. Being a woman and Black at every moment in my life, I felt the need for a new vision of the world that included not only Black people's and working people's rights, but also the full and equal participation of women. So it was imperative that the fight be carried on, on this front also. As well, I began to make a clear linkage between the specificity of people's lives and the power structures. I made specific connections between oppression of women and imperialism, creating new awareness. Whereas most art reflects or carries consciousness, my poetry began to create consciousness.

ITT ALCAN KAISER
Canadian Imperial Bank Of Commerce
privilege names in my country
but I am illegal here

I came to Canada and found
the doors of opportunity well guarded

— Lillian Allen,
  "I Fight Back"

My work became so eclectic that I was invited to read at many different events by many different groups — labour unions, schools, cultural and community events, universities, art groups, women's conferences, folk festivals, new music festivals and women's festivals, literary groups, Black heritage classes, libraries, weddings, nightclubs, not to mention the never-ending demand for benefits, rallies and political demonstrations. Sometimes my poetry presentation would be the keynote speech at an event.

Publishing was another story. *Rhythm & Hardtimes* was the first published book to include dub poetry in Canada. It was self-published and distributed, and this experience demystified the publishing process for many who had not considered publishing as an option before.

Seven self-published books immediately followed. Several more have been published since. Some of these books have sold in the thousands. *Rhythm & Hardtimes* itself sold over 8,000 copies.

The marriage of dub and music was not always an easy or happy one, because dub poets worked primarily with the word, in a form that was already complete by the time we entered the collaborative process with musicians. Years of experimentation with music and musicians were rewarded in 1985 when I brought together a fine group of grassroots reggae musicians, along with members of Canada's new top pop group, the Parachute Club, to produce *Revolutionary Tea Party*, an album that won Canada's 1986 Juno Award for best reggae/calypso album. My second album, *Conditions Critical*, released in 1988, also won a Juno award. The albums propelled dub poetry beyond the bounds of literary or arts communities into the mass of pop culture.

The accessibility of dub poetry is one reason for its cross-appeal. The political subject matter is relevant to most of the world's population. Dub poetry validates the lives and aspirations of those ignored and excluded from the dominant culture. It articulates a just vision of the future. It carries a spirit of defiance, celebration and empowerment. There is a spiritual connection because it asserts revolutionary possibilities — most importantly for those who must struggle for freedom and transformation.

The first generation of dub poets wrote of police brutality, of dashed immigrants' dreams, of hard work and little pay, of the oppression of Black women at the hands of Black men, of the need to nurture and fight back. We made art part and parcel of political work.

In May, 1993, in Toronto the first International Dub Poetry Festival brought together over one hundred dub poets from over twenty countries around the world including practitioners from Canada's First Nations community, Ethiopia, South Africa, the U.S., France and Germany to reveal that dub poetry has only just begun and is already a growing international phenomenon.

Because dub poetry is not strictly pagebound, and because institutions in our society do not account for our existence, we have gone directly to the public, recording, performing and self-publishing. We sidestepped the all-powerful "middleman" who serves as the arbiter of culture. Dub poets — with their activism and solidarity work, a network of readings and poetry across the country, and a political stance and media profile — have emerged as a major national Black cultural presence in Canada. Dub poets have galvanized a movement of Black culture, of Black writers and a progressive culture of resistance in Canada, and have set a standard for political art unparalleled in this country.

Lillian Allen
Toronto, 1993

She would sing liberation

Nellie Belly Swelly

Nellie was thirteen
don't care 'bout no fellow
growing in the garden
among the wild flowers

she Mumma she dig & she plant
nurtures her sod
tends her rose bush
in the garden pod

lust leap the garden fence
pluck the rose bud
bruk it ina the stem

oh no please no
was no self defence
oh no please no
without pretence
offered no defence
to a little little girl
called Nellie

Nellie couldn't understand
Mr. Thompson's hood
so harsh, so wrong
in such an offensive

Nellie plead, Nellie beg
Nellie plead, Nellie beg
but Mr. Thompson's hood
went right through her legs

knowing eyes blamed her

Nellie disappeared from sight
news spread wide
as the months went by
psst psst psst Nellie belly swelly
Nellie belly swelly Nellie belly swelly
children skipped to Nellie's shame

Nellie returned from the night
gave up her dolls
and the rose bush died
Nellie Momma cried Nellie Momma cried
little Nellie no more child again

No sentence was passed
on this menancing ass
who plundered Nellie's childhood

In her little tiny heart
Nellie understood war

She mustered an army within her
strengthened her defence
and mined the garden fence

No band made a roll
skies didn't part
for this new dawn
infact, nothing heralded it
when this feminist was born

My Momma

When it came to being revolutionary
my Momma she stood up for us
she would fight off a bus

Papa breaks limits
screech skid marks in our minds
aiming to make ladies of us
hold us back in time

my sister Doreen she was greedy
and liked only girls
my father didn't mind
or thought nothing unkind
boys were too much like him
sadocentric and potent

my Momma she was pregnant every year or so
bore us twelve sibilies
six girls in a row
she scrubbed floors
washed and hung miles and miles of clothes
got pregnant again
my mother, pregnant was her biggest event

she left my father
for Kate Millett, Angela Davis and the North Star
for the first time in her life

she would sing liberation
and live with it
               (swing low sweet chariot
                        step it 'gainst babylon)

my Momma she said freedom
was buying steak if she wanted
without asking anyone
It was wearing her skirt on her knees
or wherever she please
without displeasing someone

watching her children grow were the chains
that kept her bold and hoping
independence severed umbilicals
and released her

my Momma she watched us get married
and divorced
fall in and out of love
and stood by us

times we pass connect join
run rings 'round each other
slip in and out of time
umbilicals reconnect
knot
through her maternal line

my Momma she say
every woman has the experience of giving all she could
and every woman knows the feeling
of having nothing left
not even for herself
women were raised to be givers
darned if we are not good

my Momma she says
any woman who can make a dot into a child
inside of her
and bring it outside to us
is a model for a revolution

my Momma
when it comes to being revolutionary
she stood up for us
and beside us

she did always say
it takes two

PO   E   3

R   h   y   t   h   m

riddim

rebel   revolt

resistance

R   e   vo   lu   t   i   on

if these words are not poetic
then poetry has no means to free me

Psychic At Twelve

The day my grandmother was pronounced dead
for the second time
I was by her side
beads of garlic crystals and I
her room unsmiling solemn sad
a scent that echoed death's resolve

In that room I felt her calling
I felt her spirit stall
no minutes entered or left the hour

my spirit took flight
clutching hers
an interlocutory curvature of the psyche
her soul urging a push
I caught her on a breeze
held her close
till she fought her way back

that year grandma lived
danced around the fire
made its flame crackle and blush

Marriage

When mi sidown
pon mi bombo claat
inna calico dress
under the gwango tree
a suck coarse salt
fi the night fi dun
wen twist face joan
an mi man mus come
down those concrete steps
from her tatch-roof house
han in han an smile
pon dem face

an a bus' im 'ead
wid a cistern brick
blood full mi yeye
a tear im shut
rip 'im pride
the little heng pon nail

the two rocky miles 'ome
we drop some fists
blood soaked licks
kasha sticks

but later on
a sooth 'im pain

bathe the blood down
the cistern drain
ten common-law-years
inna wi tenament yard

an sure as 'ell
wi anger rest
'im eyes regret
plea 'an confess
then 'im glide mi
to gramma dead-lef bed
an' marry mi
under the chinnelle spread
again an' again
till day does done
evening come

Feminism 101

Instead of being the doormat
get up and be the door

Good Womanhood
(Censorship)

She builds her life
the latest TV shows
tailored emotions
rock 'n' roll radio

was the woman
a good woman should be
laboured at work
her boss' dream
laboured at home
no life
time of her own
lived through her man
like only good women can

then the children came
and the smile and the charm
and the goodness of her heart
could no longer hold together
the shattering parts

and he would beat her
when she screams
he say he'd kill her

twenty-five years
she balanced that life
knife-edge of good womanhood

then the civil rights movement came
opened up a door
Black peoples' and women's movements came
it opened up some more

she took a class
joined a club
got involved for the first time
on the picket lines

at the age of fifty-nine
climbed out of sublime

and that song of Bob Marley rattles in her head
'ah feel like bombing a church when I found out
the preacher was lying'

and she found out the TV was lying
and she found out the newspaper was lying
and she found out the government is lying
at the age of fifty-nine
a woman in her prime
like a river up a mountain
where the sun explodes
climbs out of sublime

and into the clearing

Women Do This
Every Day

Nine months outa de year
a woman in labour
if it was a man
a bet they woulda paid her

The Subversives

You have abstracted from me
        an abstraction of your likeness
piled bouquets of approval at my feet

You made me a uniform
        a place in line
         stick me in the dictionary
legitimize your understanding

I exist as a definition
        intransitive verb in a line
           I break from your sentence

              write a paragraph of my own

              create new forms

          space

dig lane ways
             jump your ratrace rides
turn gutters into trenches

Ida is a higgler in the market place
Rita a drummer in the band
Heather is part of the Incite collective
Sheila a woman identified woman

You have taken my abstractions
broken my images
carved images-of-broken on my mirror
data process needs
package dreams on TV
separate me from self
race   gender
              history

We who create   space
who transform what you say   is
                          send you scurrying
                          scurrying to the dictionary
to add   new words

We, we are the subversives
We, we are the underground

Sheroes, dreams & history

Tribute To Miss Lou

HEARTBEAT
Pred out yuself Miss Lou
Lawd, yu mek wi heart pound soh
yu mek wi just love up wiself
an talk wi talk soh

spirit words
on a riddim fire
word flame beat
pumps de heart
pulses history's heat

She writes
the heartbeat of our lives
dignity/culture/politics/history/lovingness/soul
dis dressup oman wi shinning star

HISTORY
Her story
my story
his story
our story
brukout story

THE VOICE

The voice
strug ug ugg uggling
to be heard

hear dis;
dem sey we sey she sey he sey hear sey
raw rim of soul
her mirror a poem
with room to grow

LANGUAGE

Get up
dance clap
sweat pon de ground
tambourine
sing a ring ding
sing a ring ding

If wi caant sing wi 'Linstead Market'
an 'Wata Com A Mi Yeye'
is what mek you gwine think
we coulda did feel satisfied

the language of the people
is the language of life

WINGS

She gives voice

       (and)   form

       (and)   wings to the silenced

"BEAR UP"

Candy Seller
how is business nowadays?
a *South Parade Peddle*   meddle
Problems   Problems
Hardtimes
Invasions
My Dreams
see *Jamaica Elevate*
Changes
bear up people for the *Victory Parade*
It Wut It   *It Wut It*

CHO MON

when Auntie Roachie speak
cho mon
oonu know sey if a noh soh
a near soh

A TRUE

And the first and last sentence
in the book of her life reads:
Jamaican people in dem free spiritidness
in dem purity
in dem Caribbeaness
in dem Blackness

in dem cunning and industriousness
in dem 'tuppidness and imperfection
is precious

and even the ugliest among us
agents of doom and exploitation
you will hear say;
'A true mon. A true thing Miss Lou a talk, yes!'

SOUL FLICKER
Sometimes, sometimes
in the midst of oppression
a soul emerges
in the dense silence
in the conspiracy of normalcy
and officialdom

sometimes in this dimness
a flicker
a light
a path
a Miss Lou

Limbo Dancer

Limbo dancer
shackles on your feet
awash   enchain
the slave ship
resist life's defeat
made your songs
chains so strong
did your dance
chained restrictions

limbo dancer
how yu carry Africa so
limbo dancer
how yu spirit strong so

uh uhu uh uhu   uh uuh uh uh

dance yu dance
prisoner in a den
dance yu dance
rise up again
oh limbo dancer
mek yu galang so   oh oh

shackles on your feet
dance on the slave ship
dance against defeat

bend bending low
bend like a willow
bending like a bow
bend bending down
back against the ground

Now tourist pay
see yu make a show
laugh
try to bend
their backs down low

Limbo dancer
like a willow
like a bow
prisoner in a den
dance yu dance
free yu Africa again

uh uhu uhu   uh uhu uh hu

Limbo in limbo
yu limbo like me
yu limbo in limbo
yu limbo to be free

To the Child

To the child who loves to sing silly songs
to the child who dresses a little weird
to the child whose heart wanders
for you I've written this poem

Not everyone can fit in a round or square
not every bird will sing a loud song
not every tree will outgrow another one
but every child can be someone

and to the child who can't always win a race
to the child who can't draw a perfect heart
to the child who has a weird little laugh
to the child who somehow stands apart

Nothing But A Hero

Harriet Tubman
you're nothing but a hero
a real cool
super duper visionary
revolutionary shero

you didn't just sit there on your bum bum bum
waiting for freedom to come come come
you got up and kicked some butt butt butt

said "It's time to let my people go
                    let 'em go, let 'em go"
so you planned the escape routes
your underground railroad

they coulda charged you with treason
but freedom and justice your reasons
nothing was gonna hold you down
nothing coulda hold you down
(When you mean business Harriet
you sure mean business)

Harriet Tubman
you're nothing but a hero
a real cool super duper
visionary revolutionary shero

You said
"Since equality under the law does not exist
... all this slavery business
slave masters ... whips
and all that shhhhhhhhh ... stuff!
I'm outta here ...
my mind is set on freedom!
freedom for my people!!!!

so you planned the escape routes
your underground railroad

they coulda charged you with treason
but freedom and justice your reasons
nothing was gonna hold you down
nothing coulda hold you down

Harriet we thank you
your skill your dedication
your lifelong determination
your love of Black people
a mind so strong and free

Harriet Tubman
you're nothing but a hero
a real cool super duper visionary
revolutionary shero

A Little Girl's Dream

Over the shadows in a moonlight
kjustu   kjustu ju ju dreams daring a mystery
sequested hues   golden spree of light
colours steal a rainbow, traces it's journey
imagined light

Mauve manoeuvers, full in the blue room
broken green of twilight
night turns day, turns night, turns light

take my soul and let it sing
take my hands and let them build
take my heart and let it heal
kjustu kjustu ju juj ju ju

Move moors, mooring morning
a light house stands guard
the sea grows calm, vex, complex
earth lay still 'neath the stares
of stars

Way out. Outside
limits of ears, eyes
limitless movement is born
grows, dances, multiplies, dies
born again, rebirth, relived, realize

Live over the moorings of planets
dreams released return. Over again and over

In the eve of youth
a child prays to be big, to be large
to be as big as the sky
oh what a day   ho ho
oh what a way hoho ho   o
O what a joy   O what a life

over the shadows in a moon light
daring a mystery   kjustu kj ustu k justu
a little girl dreams

The Day Mandela Was Released From Jail

The day Mandela was released from jail
my mother cried. She cried and cried
I watched her wondering
I asked her why
she said she felt the pain of all black people
of those who died struggling
She felt the pain of each and everyone
sentenced 'cause the colour of their skin
sentenced 'cause of racism
And yes this is one bright hopeful day
and yes it is a joy to celebrate
and now can never be too late
the toll it wrecks is way too great
and somehow it made her cry
made my mother cried and cried
so much pain for those still struggling
for very simple things in life
like the right to vote
the right to work
the right to our land
and the right to lead a dignified life

And yes it was a time to celebrate
one bright and joyful day
Oh Malcolm can you hear me

Sojourner, your truth
Martin there's an empty chair beside me
Zora Neale Hurston it's sure lonely without you

Yes for all black people
today is a very special day
and for those who love peace and justice
in every way
today a celebration for Mandela
tomorrow we're further on the way
freedom from apartheid in South Africa
freedom any which way

Liberation

You speak as if my liberation
is a one-way fare
you act as if my liberation
is some ill retreat
with naked bodies
and wooden dolls
well try to take your hand from your blinded eyes

You say I should not try to undo
the image you hold of me
does it shake your world when I start to undo
your image of what I should do
the aged myths in which you have hidden me
it's time to take your hands from your blinded eyes

My friend, my liberation
didn't come from imagining
my friend, my liberation
didn't come from chasing dreams
there was hunger silence sweat
it's time to take your hands from your blinded eyes

All I am declaring
is that I have the same right
to be myself as you do
colour my own image as you do
yes I have the same right

to live for myself as you do
to find my way as you do
to make mistakes as you do
yes I have the same right

Somewhere in this silvered city

With Criminal Intent

They wrapped their hatred around him
a hollow tip dum de dum dum dum
blow his black head to pieces
since he was just a blackity black black blackkk
wohoose tight minds into blackout
into thinking that everytime they see we
one of us
they have to account to a soul
brutality deception crunched into centuries
the horror the horror the horror

If we could just dance
and disappear
blunt instruments that plowed the fields
served the plantations
this house of capitalist plenty
that jack and every jack one a we build
no Jackman want to say it was built
by plunder, exploitation, murder, bondage and rape
making the Black print blue
and even losing that too

They carried their hatred, psychic scar
cocked on a trigger
set to blow away forever
a black boy's right to exist, to justice, to imperfection

On a dowdy Mississauga street in December '88
just after Christmas
and you know what Christmas is like
all that good cheer and so much greed
the Kangaroos struck
black blackity black black black blackkk blackout

A cowardly aim
a decidedly, deliberate, privately purchased
banned, illegal bullet
and you don't have to join the ku klux klan anymore

They wrapped their hatred around him
heaped up bursting out
they had to let it off somewhere
and since you and you and you and you were out of sight
they hurled spite on this young son
and blow his blackity black black blakkk head to pieces
black blackity blackity blackity blackity blackkk
blackout

I tell you
justice is swift
with a fullness of criminal intent
at the end of an illegal bullet
when you face your serve and protectors
your jury, your executioner and judge

Riddim An' Hardtimes

An' him chucks on some riddim
    an' yu hear him say
        riddim an' hardtimes
        riddim an' hardtimes

music a prance
dance inna head
drumbeat a roll
hot like lead

Mojah Rasta gone dread
natt up natt up
irie
red

riddim a pounce wid a purpose
Truths and Rights
mek mi hear yu

drum
drum drum
drumbeat
heart beat
pulse beat
drum

roots wid a Reggae resistance
riddim
noh Dub them call it
riddim an' hardtimes

dem pounce out the music
carv out the sounds
hard hard
hard like lead
an it bus im in im belly
an' a Albert Johnson
Albert Johnson dead
dead
dead

but this ya country hard eh?
ah wey wi come ya fa?
wi come ya fi better
dread times
Jah signs

drum beat drum beat
pulse beat
heart beat
riddim an' hardtimes
riddim an' hardtimes

riddim an' hard
                    hard
                    hard

Without A Home

I rushed to get out of the cold one day
headed for my car
rounded the corner
piece of cardboard shuffled and fall
I looked to see what t'was moving
an' yet to my surprise
a woman sat in the alley way
a woman, her bags, her life

She had no home she had no home
this woman she had no home
no place to lie no warm inside
this woman she had no home

I sat in my office looking at the snow
see it piling high
thinking I need a much warmer coat
to face the great outside
saw a man pulling a mountain
society's cast off load
no job, no social security, no permanent abode

He had no home, he had no home
this man he had no home
no place to lie no warm inside
this man he had no home

Went to the mall the other day
shopping with vengence and greed
oh we're so unbothered
all filling our needs
so much to choose from shoppers
so much to pick and feast
so much to buy on credit
so many no basic needs

so many among us
so many left to roam
so many from the corners of our eyes
look around   look around
no place to turn
just a rotten piece of the pie

Social Worker

                        you see, my job is to explain our
policy
            i   don't make them
i just apply them
whose side are you on anyways
                i ' m just doing my job. i like you
people

            whose side are you on

            we don't have a policy to deal with your er...r
request

whose side are you on

                                    i like you
people

if only life could conform to policy manuals

oh yea?

the system would work just fine if some persons
weren't human

fit   fit   fit
          fit et et et   in
a little square
a computer printout page
fit

say she was a social worker
          but she was just a disciple from hell
               say she came to save the people
                   but could hardly

save herself

Unnatural Causes

WOOooooooooOOOoooooo

The wind howled and cussed
it knew no rest
when it ran free it was a hurricane
to be watched and silenced

silence makes you sit and rot
even cactus fades
against persistent drought

they hope the poor will become acclimatized
see how they look at skyrises
and call them mountain peaks
see how the sun greets them first
in the city
makes a rolling shadow

bong ... bong ... bong ... bong ... bong ...

Somewhere in this silvered city
hunger rails beneath the flesh
... and one by one, they're closing shops
in the city
... the Epicure, the Rivoli on the Porch ...

No small affair
... No small affair — the sequel ... Le Petit Café
the Bamboo ...

The city, a curtained metropolitan glare
grins a diamond sparkle sunset
it cuts a dashing pose

"The picture you sent on the post card
was wonderful!
It reminded me of a fairyland
where everything is so clean
a place where everyone is happy
and well taken care of
... and the sky ... the sky ... it seems so round, so
huge
and so indifferent"

Indifference passes through the wind
the wind, it rains a new breed
breeds a new passion
the passion of inaction
the inaction of politicians
the art of avoiding issues
the issues of culture
the culture of exclusion
the exclusion of the 'political'
and the powerless
bong ... bong ... bong ... bong ... bong ...

Somewhere in this our city
in our governing chambers
a watershed of indelight
of neutered niceties, unctuous
Click///click///click

postcard perfect

Dry rivers in the valley
the thirst at the banks of plenty
the room at the street-car shelter
a bus stop bed
     a bus stop bed
         a bus stop bed

You can make it through winter if you're ice
You can make it through winter if you're ice

gone frozen
on many things
bare back. no shelter
ice hearts in the elements
impassioned is the wind

All people are created equal except in winter
All people are created equal except in winter

Right here
on the front steps of abundance
Caroline Bungle tugs her load
stalks a place, invites a little company of sleep

unclick///
this my dear is very unpostcardlike

Not inclined to poses
posturing only her plight
a dungle of terror
of lost hope
abandonment
an explorer in the arctic of our culture
a straggler adrift
cross our terrain of indifference
a life unravelled
seeks a connection
a soul outstretched to the cosmos

Can you spare a little social change, please?
a cup of tea
a place to sleep
a job
     a job
          a job ...????

"The last postcard you sent was kinda weird
... poor people, sleeping at the bus stop!??
Surely you don't have that there ..."

"... anyways, I'm dying to come to Canada
I'm a pioneer!"

The Refugee

Silence rocks the night
nerve stretch tight
snapping left and right
anger peels ...
a straight faced appeal
to the Canada that can
to save him

no one appeared
or dared to care
for the solitary heart
that paced the night

morning brought light
more panic and fright
for the vacant of days
that faced him

he ran from the light
took a balcony dive
plunges his life
to the pavement below
that plagued him

nothing resolved
a few problems got solve
two months rent defrayed

the credit companies got swayed
on his apartment a sign says
Now Renting

Dark Winds

Dark winds choked on the icy air
frustration was breathing
pleasure found ease
in the music beating pounding
bass line driving stroving
slap to the guitar hot licks
stirring up a musical commotion
the notion is rebel reggae rebel motion

Man and woman and youth and I one
seeped in a voyage of discovery
a mystic deep black journey
the denseness and the blackness of the glory
glowing shining
the past and the present well aligning

What the people have to do nowadays mi say
if them work hard in a dance hall, ina house yard
ina school yard
just a uggle fi get a little space

and the haste and the waste
how them lay them bare
cause them black, cause them black
and the system justa progress pon them back
pon them back

and de music jus a beat
an the dance hall a rock
yu coulda just hear
the feeling of gladness
mixed with hope jus a crackle
and the music jusa beat
in the heat of de sweat
and the tiredness and emptyness regress

Delroy and Imogene stood by the wall
cotch it up like if them move it woulda did drop
roll a crackle anda clap
a youth mouth burn;
"riddim! journey forward"

and the p'lice them outside
couldn't stand the noise
that the heat and the beat and the mystic mists
was a blowing winds of glory
in a reggae creation story

and BAM!
them kick down the door
put everyone pon the floor
face down flat, face down flat

It was a brutal attack
pon the spirit of survival
pon the culture and the spirit of revival
pon de youth of Jane & Finch
cause them black, cause them black

what the people have to do today mi say
just a uggle fi get a little peace
and the haste and the waste
how them lay them bare
cause them black cause them black
cause the system just a progress pon them back
pon the back

But our youths of today
just haffi find a way
fi stand them ground
and fight back
and fight back
and fight back.

His Day Came

They came for him that day
and sure as hell they found him

He wasn't even watching tv

His principal said he was a disgrace
disgrace
a discredit to his race
His mother she worked hard
she worked hard
and prayed

She got him everything he wanted
she bought him a colour tv
an Atari computer a five-speed bicycle
and a three-piece suit
but he wanted her to stop slaving
working in some white man's factory
stop slaving working in some white man's factory

His principal Mr. Frazer said
his mother was a hard-working woman
quite happy and
well suited to her job

That's when he smashed his fist
into Mister Fraser's face

He sent the principal's dentures
flying flying
He said it was the biggest
most dirty lie he's ever heard
(The biggest most trucking dirty lie
he's ever heard)

So they came for him that day
and sure as hell they found him

And leaving like that
in the back of a police cruiser
wasn't easy
The tears cracked crackled
like a rock inside of him
and the policeman asked him if
he was feeling any pain

(Are you feeling pain, boy?
Are you feeling pain?
Are you feeling pain, boy?
Are you feeling pain?)

He only replied
looking thin through thin air
thinness a picture
in front of him
God please help Mama
God please help Mama
God please
God please

God God ...
God

They came for him that day
and sure as hell they found him ...

Rub A Dub Style Inna Regent Park

Monday morning broke
news of a robbery
Pam mind went
couldn't hold the load
dem took her to the station
a paddy wagon
screaming ...
her Johnny got a gun
from an ex-policeman

Oh Lawd, Oh Lawd Oh Lawd eh ya
a wey dis ya society a do
to wi sons

Rub a dub style
inna Regent Park
mon a dub it inna dance
inna Regent Park
oh lawd oh lawd

"forget yu troubles and dance"
forget yu bills them
an irie up yuself
forget yu dreams gathering dusts
on the shelves

dj rapper hear im chant
pumps a musical track
for im platform
cut it wild
sey de system vile
dubbing it inna dance
frustration pile
a different style
inna regent park

could have been a gun
but's a mike in his hand
could've been a gun spilling out the lines
but is a mike
    is a mike
        is a mike
Oh Lawd Oh Lawd Oh Lawd

riddim line vessel im ache
from im heart outside
culture carry im past
an steady im mind
man tek a draw an feeling time
words cut harsh   try to find
explanations
de sufferings of de times

"forget yu troubles and dance"
forget yu bills dem
an irie up yu self
forget yu dreams gatherin

dust   dust   dust

is a long time wi sweating here
is a long time wi waiting here
to join society's rites
is a long time wi beating down yu door

is a long time since wi mek the trip
cross the Atlantic
on the slave shippppppppp
is a long long time wi knocking
an every time yu slam the door
sey: no job
discrimination injustice
a feel the whip lick
an is the same boat
     the same boat
        the same boat
Oh Lawd   Oh Lawd   Oh Lawd   eh ya

dj chant out cutting it wild
sey one hav fi dub it inna different style
when doors close down on society's rites
windows will prey open
in the middle of the night
dashed hopes run wild
in the middle of the night
Oh Lawd   Oh lawd   Oh Lawd   eh ya

*D*is

Dis Word

dis word breeds my rhythm
dis word carries my freedom
dis word is my hand
:   my weapon

21 Footnotes

If I take away your twenty-one footnotes
can your ideas lean
pon dis ya dis ya hungry belly
will it anchor the struggling soul
be a foothold to empower
will it echo resistance like a dream when I tap
or will it hang like a Botticelli on the wall
or just an accordion fold and collapse

I Dream a Redwood

Last night I dream I was a Redwood
on the mountain side
a thousand three hundred years old
breathe out pure oxygen
working morning and night
for this beautiful planet
all for life

I dream people love and admire me
say how wondrous this world
trees animals, persons and things
can all live

I wish you were a Redwood
how great we would understand
the love and care it takes
to appreciate this land

I dream you were beside me
standing tall and growing strong
the earth we share
flesh dirt and spirit
is our bond

Oh oh to be a wise old Redwood
a great big heart of wood
oh oh to be a Redwood

dreaming
dreaming tales

Born To Log

legend of broken treaties
wounded trees
wounded land
chaka chaka
lumberjack(al) iron paws
corporate arm(ies)
wages war on sacred territory

keepers of the faith
lay their bodies on the line
levity's breath steals
across lines
a rueful landscape of plunder
sylphs rustle with leaves

an ex-hippie sprinkles her blessings
on the land and apologises;
"Mother Earth, Trees ... forgive us
I am so sorry"

the government proclaims;
"With our laws and our armies
we must defend the logging companies right
to destroy everything in sight
they've paid for it
and they create jobs jobs jobs"

a protestor prays aloud
dragged away chaka chaka
big iron in the forest
chaka chaka
"For all the things on the earth
that cannot speak
cannot defend their lives
the wild ones
the wolves, trees, insects
for all the little tiny things
organisms unknown ..."

and a logger yells;
"Get them away ... I have to do my job
like I do everyday
this is my work my livelihood"
as if to say ...
born to log

the old woman naturalist amazed
"What a destiny —
to chop down virgin forests"
saw his heart
chain saw chaka chaka

and the poets chant;
"Jobs won't solve all our problems
we should hug old grandma grandpa trees
not log them"

Why Do We Have To Fight

Why do we have to fight
for what is our natural rights
no change without struggle
no one in power ain't giving up nuttin

yu born yu live an then yu die
inbetween yu dodge the dubious lies
oh where is the promised pie
where is the carrot for the taking

Why do we have to fight
for what is our natural rights
no change without struggle
no one in power ain't giving up nuttin

a woman's work is not recognized
if she be black makes it doubly-dized
without a man she's in nothing's land
why do we have to fight for a place to live
this is the society that our toil has built
what would it take to make
a home a right
what would it take to legalize

why do we have to fight?

Battle Scars

(for Ruth)

Oh sister yu looking weary
oh sister yu looking worn
oh sister yu seeming harried
oh sister I see you strong

fought for women's rights
in the trenches
waged battle on and on
many things
we now take for granted
were hard won

For all our gains
you bore the pain
for all the pain
you bore the cost

Feminism from the trenches
broke the chains
and rush the fences
we feel reinvented
tired but strengthened
women lives changing the world
medals for your battle scars

A Peace to Swallow

peace woke up one morning
looked for a table to break fast
there was no room at the inn
no in into the innercircle
no one to break bread
but those whose plates were empty
What is peace anyway, but rich man's poison!

Dis Ya Mumma Earth
(Peace Poem)

Dis ya dis ya mumma earth
is wi home land
dis ya dis ya mumma earth
is wi only one

all lovers of the earth
nuclear arms protesters, anti-war activists
liberation fighters
we are the poets
restless
the summer's sun
spreading de warmth
spreading de word
inna dis ya dis ya mumma earth
cause everything pon it
wi blood an sweat in it
is fi everybody homeland
all a fi wi own

get up stand up
shout en masse
wail in the wilderness
our will …will be
peace … justice … equality
join hands in liberation dance

freedom chants
we are our only weapons for peace
people/demonstrations/banners/chants
linking arms
fight if we must
fight/fight
listen to the poets chant
listen to the people's wants
peace ... peace ... peace

dis ya dis ya mumma earth
is wi homc land
dis ya dis ya mumma earth
is wi only one

Conditions Critical

Border Crossings

They found them as they waited for a coyote
a dingy rundown hotel room
they sold the farm, the broken down family car
headed north in a forest of hope
they carried a suitcase without a past
twin baby girls and their little boy

I've dreamt this dream for my family
we have no way to live here
we dearly love our country
we can't fill our stomach on political dictates

It's very scary

Thinking of all the difficulties ahead
but we have to take the risk
stand up and organize
hope that faith is with us
and vindicates us on the other side

it's a dangerous moment when we decide to leave
it's a dangerous moment when we cross
in a dangerous moment living as we do
it's a dangerous moment getting caught

Standing at the cross roads
centuries on your chest

U. S. might strung 'round your neck
will she come
can your youth be returned
can your land be returned

Will you ever whisper her name
freedom

Nicaragua

I can tell the flames of a secret fire
flaring Sandanista's courage
I can see in the darkened bushes
smell the freshness of an idea taking root
I can make my way through the darkness
looking is just *one* way to see

I can sense another language
another intention
another story that will tell itself
make the world new

There is something from this journey
makes me stand up
makes my legs strong

There is a watering hole
way in the souls of men and women
who dare to sstt — struggle
(uggle to struggle to uggle to struggle)

There is a language that's universal
that's known through the ages
whispered in the streets
and shouted in houses
there is a spirit that unites us in *revolution*

I shall always remember yours days of bravery
and sadness
I shall always remember your joy
I shall always remember your deliberate
and spontaneous intentions
the love that flourishes in the souls of your people
Nicarauga
I shall always remember
I know

Freedom Is Azania
(South Africa Must Be Free)

Nerves twang fears sharpen
discord grows
in South Africa
where they don't need a reason
to oppress you
'cept the colour of your skin
bronze blakk
'cept you're African and Bantu
Xhosa spirited
'cept it's your country
and that's where you're gonna die anyway
they feel it in your daring
as they psychopathicly rewrite your history

you feel your back crack ... crackkk ... cracking
your arms and legs
and spirits growing strong
four hundred years of resistance crystallize
        you will not lie down
                you will not lie down

In South Africa hope pounds endlessly
                in a drumbeat rage
grandmothers carry their quiet breathing
fire hope

hooking the network of resistance
threads
every leaf that moves in the night
building a tapestry of voices
soft determined unshakable

In South Africa they don't need a reason to shoot
freedom cries are answered with gunshotblasts
defiant youths dragged through streets
trailing in what's left of the blood
that's been sucked from their veins for centuries

In South Africa
where decency, basic human rights
and the people's will for a just society
are swept in the garbage bin of oppression
even then fighting spirits will rise ... arise
refuse to lie down
an amputated arm will offer itself
to an old lady in the night
smuggling food to frontline fighters
a dead leg will rush off to the bush
to conspire for ancestral revenge

In South Africa
they don't need a reason to oppress you
'cept diamond gold greed superexploitation
racism capitalism imperialism
... and an unnerving fear
of the spirit of the people
standing on sixty million feet

alive
      defiant
            and swelling in resistance
Freedom is Azania   Freedom is Azania

(They can't kill the spirit)

Could It Happen In America

It was 1999 in America
the great crowd stood by the wall
though it wasn't all that visible
it separated the rich from the poor
they stood and they said no more
in our time poverty must end
they shook and the rumblings
from the things that they said
the wall came tumbling down

could it happen
happen in America
could the people file free in the streets
could we impeach the entire congress
could the voiceless now speak
could we reorganize the political system
to meet each and every need
could the poor see prosperity in America
and could we all be free

could it happen
happen in America
could the walls come tumbling down
could it happen in our lifetime
could we do it, our wills, our sound

could we march through the streets
could we stand by the wall
could we all be there and sounding the call

could it happen
happen in America
could the wall of poverty fall

Dictator
(for Haiti)

the dust that makes you will someday
turn to mud in the rain
and fertilize land for the peasants
its fruit shall bear no resemblance of you
only a song of the past about evil days
long gone
shall we remember your name
dictator

Conditions Critical

Dem a mash it up down inna Jamaica
dem a add it up down inna Jamaica
dem a mash it up down inna Jamaica
dem a add it up down inna Jamaica

gas prices bounce
hoops for the skies
a likkle spark and the embers of oppression
rise
people tek to the streets
it's no negotiating stance

when do yu want freedom?
yesterday!
how do you propose you'll get it?
by the people's way!

soh, that's why ...
dem a mash it up down inna Jamaica
dem a add it up down inna Jamaica

dem sey dem tired of trying to buy the country back
from the Americans and the IMF pact
a little friendly debt with an open end
it feel like the ball and chain game again

soh, that's why ...
dem a mash it up down inna Jamaica
dem a add it up down inna Jamaica
conditions critical
freedom has been mythical

every few years years a new deliverer come
say 'better must come, let *me* lead the way my people'

seems better get delayed
somewhere hiding
it's quarter to twelve
an' it's getting late

better change to waiting
an' we waiting here a while
an' the weight
is piling on our backs
we sweating and dying
under disparity's attacks, attacks attacks

an' our children still bawling
our ancestors still calling
an' wi right ya soh demanding

soh, that's why ...
dem a mash it up down inna Jamaica
dem a add it up down inna Jamaica
conditions critical
freedom has been mythical
conditions critical

ecliptical
critical

The life of a sound

One Poem Town

Hey!   Hey!   Hey!
this is a one poem town
this is a one poem town

ride in on your macrame verses
through barber-green minds
keep it kool! kool! kool!
on the page
'cause, if yu bring one in
any other way
we'll shoot you with metaphors
tie you cordless
hang you high in ironies
drop a pun 'pon yu toe
and run you down, down, down
and out of town
'cause, this is a one poem town

and hey! what yu doing here anyway?

so don't come with no pling, ying, jing
ding something
calling it poetry
'cause, this is a one poem town
and you're not here to stay

Are you?

I Am Africa

I
    dream
        like no one
                heart
can   hold   warm
breaths of   sun

I   feeeeeel   music

my body carries the rhythms
of A   F   R   I   C   A
        sweet
rising crest of strength & laughter
Black souls swell with her song
      FREEDOM, she sings
hear   her   calling
you now

and when the music finds its source
      it   play s
        through me   l
                d
my   heart   beats   i
             p
        a
      r
I and Africa are one

Anti-Social Work

Fit   Fit

Fffit   Fffit   Fffit

it   it   it   it   it   it
Fff   f   f   Fff   ttttttt
Fi ie   e   it
      FIT

      FI

      F
F   Fff   Fff ff

FFF   F
f
It It et
eTTTT
EBEEEEEEEEEEEEEEEEEEERE

FIT   IT   HIT   fit it it it

Antifit   anti-FIT

anti   SO · C · I · AL
                    (work)

Jazz You

Molten shimmer red
charcoal roasting
like hot, burn
burn black, burn sax
burn blue
burn into my flesh
brewing a potpourri of a storm
ablowing waves of hues

hot wax, rise
and sink
twist
and sizzle in the frying pan
mood simmer
agasp
gasp, gasp gasp
gasping ... oh yea

a breath in the life of a sound
breezes through sax
breathes jazz, breathes sax
a step to beat prap ... pa ... pa ... pap

my heart was your whipping stick
oh heart
and your soul, my tambourine

shake, shake on
shake life into them silent sounds
solo in duet
solo on the breeze
volar solar ing
be you be bird be song
sing
sing the ba luse
sing blue skies
sing me
sing you skies
sing oh oh, oh sway, oh stay
ooh oh ooOOoo

sing me you
sing the go away frustration blues
sing I ain't stop singing till I trucking
through blues

the notes and the melodies keep, slip
sa lip sa lippling
oh real so real surreal
slip
oo so tired
and there's no music in dem here toes
music, no music, oh music, the music
always
the music

To a Jazz Musician (Contemplating Suicide)

In the beginning was a lone jazz musician
played the first note
nucleus of the sun began to take
rippled off a few bars
layers of mountains came dancing
the tune got spicier
waterfalls broke through
slowed and got spacy
the atmosphere took its place
movement and timing
separated night from day
the music played and the song diffused
trees flowers rivers and seas took roots
In the beginning the Jazz musician played
didn't put that instrument down
until the seventh day

Jazz musician you are your notes and knows
and knows not
mind cannot comprehend limits of structure
time and space intrude
when rhythms of creation pulse through you
spiced by your impulse,
let's commit Jazz

Ja/Ja/Ja/Ja   Jazz
create a new universe
in here
out there
somewhere!
Ja/Ja/Ja/Ja   Jazz

Another Jazz Poem

fools don't rush in
core key keeping
improv is sen say tonal
you called begged music
for words
beckon faith
a leap   drift note   half note
taa tap ta tee

painted mercurial moodtalk
e mo tonal
expresses vis a vis
in/off key
chordial   lang use   age
unchord   inner   language
music ain't music till you play
(yu hear)

sync styming groove
carries follows leads
d   i   s   s   i   p   a   t   e   s
spin
stars in the cosmos
planet out of orbit
chase tha groove
lead tha groove
find tha groove

chase tha groove
lead tha groove
find tha groove

genius! they say
O   Gggggggeee!
mind ignores barriers
flows floods
comprehend way out   outside
distant reaches of the universe
kapto symphonic soundcliptical
rhythmic   fire

who knows what's driving those fingers
what storm lurks in a sax player's lungs

the music is   becomes
new life
formal   inert   nonformal
matter
but does it matter, really?

the universe grows
in fi nite
in de fi nite
infinitismal
cosmosymphonic
intervention
unexpectational
genius   oh genius
O G

you've added sparkles
of spiritual inertia
to our universe

who we touch   touch deep
heart transmit lazer roo
full fully unawares
a fine tune
wings
if you can make tears roll from our eyes
jazz musician
if you can make us cry
you can make us fly

music I come to you like a watering hole
sip/gulp/gapple/gasp
ripples skip out from my lips
watch those circles start up and grow
wonder just where those circles go

So What
(Perspective Poem)

So what so what so what
So your years of schooled craft
have created fine poems
so it ended pollution
so it stopped wars
so it fed starving children
so it gave life to the dying
so it brought peace to one single land
so no one should imperil its form
so if you're high up in a poetic fiefdom
so, so self assured and turgid
so what if I write a poem like a song

A Poem Against Things

There is no other time or place
to sing   tear up a book
or write a poem

Land so strange a dream
work day after day
another constructed smile
another wretched penny saved

I write poems
like a weapon
oh why oh why
and when will it end

Thursdays I meet
planning protest
slavery's ghost rise up
fury in their heads

War dance on Ottawa, Washington
brothers sisters wrestle
South Africa to the ground
bury apartheid dead

Morning pulls the dawn
from deep South African nights
Azania strong and free

There is no other time or place
to sing
tear up a book
or write a poem
but here and now

A mek wi

Revolutionary Tea Party

You who know what the past has been
you who work in the present tense
you who see through to the future
come mek wi work together

come sit here with we
a mek wi drink tea
a mek wi talk
a mek wi analyse

You who have been burned by vanguardism
come mek wi give yu little nurturing
come sit awhile
a mek wi drink tea
a mek wi talk
a mek wi strategize

You who believe in the future
in transforming by your labour
let the future be in good favour

We who create the wealth of the world
only get scrapings from them in control
when wi siddown and look at the system
check out the way that things been
wi haffi say ... wi haffi say
the system in a really bad way

A wey it a defend?

You who see for peace a future
you who understands the past
you who create with yu sweat from the heart
let's talk, let's make art, let's love, dance
revel in the streets if that's the beat
protest demonstrate chant

You who see for us a future
come sit here with we
mek wi drink tea
mek wi talk
mek wi analyse
mek wi strategize
mek wi work together

Liberation Comes

liberation comes slowly
sometimes
a burglar in your sleep
       a crack
           doubt
                an affirmation

peek on possibilities
and answers will come   barefoot

                 and
naked
prop on your door step
            and beat at your door

if you open to peek

it rushes in
like a flood

down a laneway

can't just ignore it like a beggar
when you go by

It's Not Apathy

for Blanche

I pause
ease the load
take a rest
a quiet inbreathe
love a little
nurture myself

battered
all these years
struggling
struggling physically
struggling mentally
struggling emotionally
struggling
struggling

it's not apathy
just want to ease the load
take a rest
close my eyes for a minute

Sister Hold On

Hold on sister
Sister hold on

I know times are tough tough tough
you work yuself to the bones to loose this rut
but Babylon system conspire to down you
remember your strength sister
remember your joys
remember you're whole sister
and you're not alone

Hold on sister
Sister hold on

I know times are rough rough rough
seems like things jus' a get worst
some moments feel like a nuclear holocaust

Hold on sister
Sister hold on

I know you got struggles sister
right up to your eyes
just wishing the pressures could ease
signal a little relief in your life
but everytime you turn around
it's another barrier to break down

just hold on sister
sister hold on

Remember your strength sister
remember those passed
you've come this far sister
hold on

I Fight Back

ITT ALCAN KAISER
Canadian Imperial Bank of Commerce
these are privilege names in my country
but I am illegal here

My children scream
My grandmother is dying

I came to Canada
found the doors of opportunity
well guarded

I scrub floors
serve backra's meals on time
spend two days working in one
twelve days in a week

Here I am in Canada
bringing up someone else's child
while someone else and me in absentee
bring up my own

AND I FIGHT BACK

And constantly they ask
"Oh beautiful tropical beach
with coconut tree and rum

why did you leave there
why on earth did you come"

AND I SAY:
For the same reasons
your mothers came

I FIGHT BACK

They label me
Immigrant, law-breaker, illegal, minimum wager
refugee
Ah no, not mother, not worker, not fighter

I FIGHT BACK
I FIGHT BACK
I FIGHT BACK

Feminism 104

revolution

Love Poem

If you wish to be a lover
if you wish to be a friend
if you wish the world be kind
to small things
if you wish hate and injustice would end
if you wish we could stand up
for all the right things
come and lie beside me
let our love be the test
and through this gift of passion
wage peace and happiness
          peace
              and
                  happiness

Birth

ah a ah   ah a ah ah aa

ah a ah   ah a ah ah aaa

ah a   ah ah a ah ah aaaa

aha   aaaaa   ahaa

an baps

                    she born

Lillian Allen moved from Spanish Town, Jamaica to North America in 1969. After studying at the City University of New York and York University in Toronto, she emerged as a birth mother of dub in Canada, performing alone and with *de dub poets* at countless events across the full spectrum of progressive organizing. She has three albums for adults and one for children, and two books for children and young people. She performs locally, nationally and internationally. A cultural strategist and long-time key cultural worker/arts activist in Toronto, Allen's also a writer of plays and short fiction and has recently ventured into filmmaking.